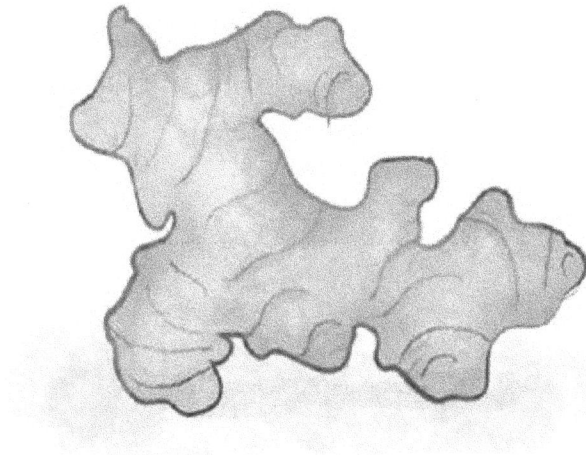

Healthy, Easy, Delicious Indian Recipes

Make Your Own Mouthwatering Indian Food with Whole, Real Food Ingredients

By Ben Hirshberg and Jessica Robinson

Illustrations by Tamara Antonijevic

Copyright © 2015 Ben Hirshberg

Go to www.BenHirshberg.com to get your free copy of The Eudaimonia Manifesto

Dedicated to the beautiful country of India, and the ingenious cooks who spent thousands of years creating the basis for the recipes included in this book.

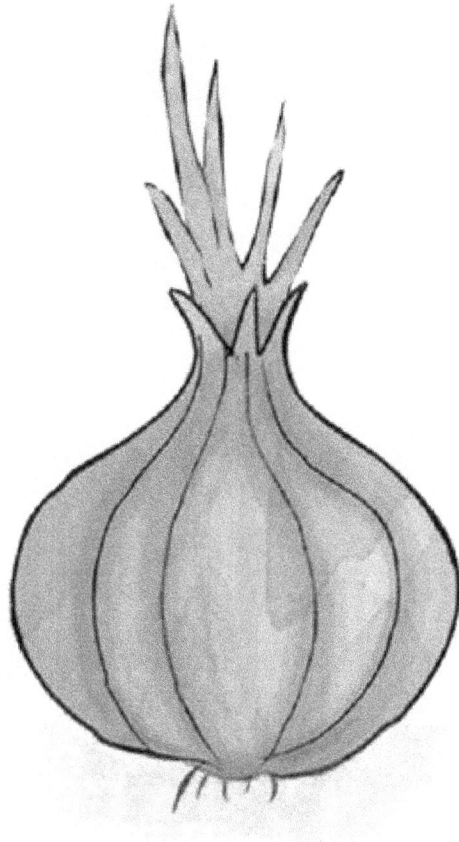

Table of Contents

Three Guiding Principles

When buying cookbooks, I look for three things in the recipes. First, they need to be easy to make. Second, they need to be healthy. Third, they need to be delicious. If a recipe can check off all three of those boxes, I consider it to be a winner.

Those same three values were what also guided the recipe creation process for this cookbook. These Indian recipes do not include any extra ingredients or steps, and are all designed to be staple meal candidates. Of course, tasting amazing was also a pre-requisite for every recipe. Lastly, every recipe in this book was created from a real-food framework, which means that they are composed of nutritious real foods, not processed, nutrient-poor foods.

A Real-Food framework is recommended by many nutrition experts, ranging from Dr. John Berardi, Dr. Andrew Weil, Dr. Drew Ramsey, Dr. Joseph Mercola, and Dr. Josh Axe, to Michael Pollen, Nina Planck, and Mark Bittman. Even health experts such as Mark Sisson, Chris Kresser, Joel Fuhrman, and David Wolfe who are on the paleo and vegan edges of the nutrition spectrum agree that a diet focused on eating whole, real foods is a healthy way to eat.

In my estimation, there are two variables that contribute to how healthy a food is: quality and preparation. A food's quality refers to how healthy a food is before any processing happens. A food's preparation refers to the steps in between a food's most raw state and the state it is in when entering our mouths. When referring to a food's quality, I am talking about how good the food is before it is cooked. Below is a list of foods and what to look for in their quality and preparation.

Keep in mind that better stuff often costs more, and **don't stress if it doesn't fit within your budget**. You're not destined to a life of sub-par health just because you can't afford organic strawberries or pastured eggs! There are many variables that determine our health, and although food preparation and quality matter, remember that they are just two variables in the large equation that determines our health.

Quality

Fish and Seafood: Wild-caught fish and seafood are generally considered to be superior to their farm-raised counterparts because of higher omega 3 fat levels and significantly lower levels of antibiotics, chemicals and other artificial contaminates. Farm-raised fish and seafood have lower levels of mercury, which is a topic of much debate among nutrition experts. I'd recommend going with wild fish and seafood because of the more favorable omega 3, antibiotic, and contamination levels.

Eggs and Poultry: Pasture-raised poultry and eggs are best, free-range is second best, and cage-free eggs take the bronze medal. Pasture-raised chickens are allowed to roam freely in their natural environment and eat their natural diet. Free-range chickens must have access to the outdoors at least 51% of the time, but there are no restrictions on what they can be fed. Cage-free chickens live in barns or warehouses, generally without access to the outdoors. The better the chicken, the more beta carotene, vitamin E, and omega 3 fat their eggs and meat will contain in addition to having lower levels of contaminates and antibiotics.

Beef, Lamb, Bison, and Dairy Products: Grass-fed and pasture-raised are the pinnacle of red meat and dairy products. These animals thrive when they are allowed to roam and eat their natural diet of green plants, but unfortunately the majority of meat and dairy products come from animals fed corn and grains while being forced into a sedentary lifestyle. Healthier ruminants have more favorable lipid profiles and are more nutrient dense, so when you eat them you should look for grass-fed and pasture-raised labels at the grocery store or farmer's market. If grass-fed, pasture-raised labels are hard to find, organic meat is a good consolation prize.

Pork: As with eggs, poultry, and red meat, pastured pork is healthiest. Feedlot pigs eat a lot of soy and corn, and pastured pigs eat roots, greens, insects, nuts, and fruits. Factory farmed pigs don't have space to move around and explore, while pasture-raised pigs do. Humans who eat well and get adequate exercise are healthier, and animals are no different. Would you rather eat healthy animals or unhealthy animals?

Preparation

Meat: Meat that is well-done or burned often has elevated levels of heterocyclic amines (HCA) and advanced glycation endproducts (AGE), which are both linked to negative health outcomes. That doesn't mean that you can't enjoy barbeque anymore though; there are a number of ways to decrease the formation of these harmful compounds. First on the list is cooking meat at a lower temperature to avoid charring and burning in the first place. The second line of defense is to marinate or rub your meat with spices, herbs, and other nutrient-dense foods. Third, eat the meat with nutrient-dense foods like vegetables, fruits, and even drinks such as red wine or coffee. All three steps have been shown to decrease HCA and AGE levels.

Dairy: The healthy preparation method for dairy that everyone can agree on is fermentation. The main benefit of fermented dairy products like yogurt and kefir is that they increase levels of healthy gut flora, which are crucial for proper digestion. Whether or not raw dairy is beneficial is under debate, however the pros appear to heavily outweigh the cons. Raw dairy detractors say that raw is far more dangerous. This is true- raw milk has a 9x greater chance of landing you in the hospital…but that 9x greater risk still only amounts to 1 in 6 million. As for the pros of non-homogenized, unpasteurized dairy? Greater levels of manganese, copper, iron, and vitamin C in addition to more bio-available vitamin A and vitamin B6. Also worth mentioning are goat dairy products, which are generally tolerated much better than cow dairy. Certainly worth a shot if you like milk, cheese, and yogurt but don't tolerate common dairy products!

Grains, Seeds, Legumes, and Nuts: Soaking and sprouting grains, seeds, legumes and nuts decreases their levels of enzyme inhibitors and phytates. Both are known to hamper our body's ability to digest and assimilate nutrients. Sprouted bread is widely available, and soaking and sprouting seeds, legumes, and nuts is fairly easy to do at home. The process is a bit different for each, but a quick Google search will give you the steps for whatever you want to soak or sprout.

Produce: Though debates rage throughout the world of nutrition, perhaps none inspire more passion than that of the GMO vs organic produce argument. Here's what I've gleaned from the research: local, fresh, organic produce is best. Fruits and vegetables are most nutritious right after harvest. As they spend days or weeks traveling across the state, country, or world, their vitamin content decreases. In addition, non-organic produce has far higher levels of pesticides, which are not proven beyond a reasonable doubt to be harmful, but still very well may have adverse effects that haven't been discovered. Ideally, we'd all get our produce from a trusted, local farm, but that isn't always possible. Although local, fresh, organic fruits and veggies are ideal, whatever you can get your hands on will still be very health promoting! Despite what GMO alarmists say, eat your vegetables, even if they aren't organic. Just be sure to wash them first to get rid of potential pesticide residue and bacteria!

Fats and Oils: The best fats and oils to cook with are coconut oil, butter, ghee, tallow, lard, and palm oil. Some oils that are okay to eat but not as good to cook with are avocado oil, macadamia nut oil, olive oil, flax oil, sesame oil and walnut oil. The first list is better to cook with because the fats are more stable, and less prone to oxidation and rancidification. Rancid, oxidized fats cause free radicals to form in our body, which are linked to heart attacks, stroke, and cancer. Oils that weren't included on either list like cottonseed oil are far too high in omega six fatty acids, too low in omega three fatty acids, and are usually heated to very high temperatures and treated with known carcinogens like hexane before being bottled. One more tip for preventing the thinner oils on the second list from oxidizing: keep them in a cool, dry, dark place. Cupboards work well in cooler climates and refrigerators work well in warmer climates.

Enjoy

Whether you are an experienced chef or an Indian food newbie, we hope you find these recipes to be as delicious, healthy, and easy to make as we do. Cheers and bon appétit!

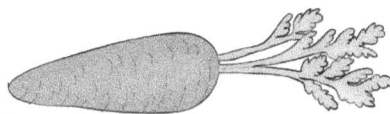

Vegetarian

Creamy Aloo Gobi

Prep Time: 10 minutes
Cook Time: 1 hour 20 minutes
Serves 4

Ingredients:

- 2 Tbsps. coconut or palm oil
- 1 medium onion, chopped
- 1 Tbsp. minced garlic
- 1 tsp. cumin seeds
- 1 (15 ounce) can diced tomatoes
- 1 cup coconut milk
- 2 Tbsps. ground coriander
- 1 Tbsp. each salt and ground turmeric
- 1 tsp. each ground cinnamon, ground ginger, ground cardamom, and cayenne pepper
- 3 large potatoes peeled and cubed
- 1 medium head cauliflower, chopped into bite size pieces
- 1 (15 ounce) can chickpeas, rinsed and drained

Directions:

1. Heat oil in a large pot on medium-high heat and add onion. Cook until softened, about 4 minutes, then stir in garlic and cumin. Continue to cook until onion begins to brown.

2. Stir in tomatoes, coconut milk, coriander, salt, turmeric, ground cinnamon, ground ginger, ground cardamom, and cayenne pepper. Stir until mixture begins to boil, then put in the potatoes, cauliflower, and chickpeas. Blend well. Reduce heat to low and cover.

3. Simmer until the potatoes are tender, 45 minutes to an hour (this will depend on the size of the potato chunks).

These Indian style potatoes and cauliflower make for a brilliant dish. These humble vegetables may not sound like much but they happen to be the perfect canvas to paint on the vibrant flavors we're using. This dish is filling without being a carb-overload and the leftovers are just as delicious for a few weekday lunches.

Creamy Coconut Indian Dahl with Spinach

Prep Time: 20 minutes
Cook Time: 30 minutes
Serves 4

Ingredients:

- 1 1/2 cups red lentils, rinsed and soaked for 20 minutes
- 3 1/2 cups water
- 1 tsp. salt
- 1/2 tsp. each ground turmeric and chili powder
- 1 pound fresh spinach, rinsed and chopped
- 2 Tbsps. ghee or butter
- 1 onion, chopped
- 1 tsp. ground cumin, mustard seed and garam masala
- 1/2 cup coconut milk

Directions:

1. Drain lentils that have been soaking for 20 minutes.

2. In a large saucepan, bring water to a boil and stir in salt, drained lentils, turmeric and chili powder. Cover and return to a boil then reduce heat to low and simmer for 15 minutes. Stir in the spinach and cook 5 minutes, or until lentils are soft. Add more water if necessary.

3. In a small saucepan over medium heat, melt ghee/butter and sauté onions with cumin and mustard seeds, stirring often. Cook until onions are transparent, and then combine with lentils. Stir in garam masala and coconut milk and cook until heated through.

Dahl is a traditional Indian dish made with lentils and spices. Lentils make this dish a healthy source of vegetarian protein while also supplying a good source of several antioxidant vitamins including vitamin C and E. We are kicking it up one more notch by adding nutrient-dense spinach to make this a power house dish of antioxidants.

Crunchy Cucumber and Peanut Salad

Prep Time: 10 minutes
Cook Time: 7 minutes
Serves 4

Ingredients:

- 2 English or other un-waxed cucumbers, chopped into 1/4" dice (about 3 cups)
- 1 medium green serrano chile pepper, finely chopped (remove seeds if desired)
- 1/2 cup raw peanuts
- 2-3 Tbsps. freshly squeezed lemon juice
- 1/4 tsp. salt
- 1/2 tsp. honey
- 1/8 tsp ground cayenne
- 1 Tbsp. palm oil
- 1/4 tsp. mustard seeds

Directions:

1. Place cucumbers and pepper in medium bowl. Using coffee grinder or food processor, chop peanuts until reduced to a coarse powder (not too fine, but no big chunks). Add to cucumbers along with lemon juice (to taste), salt, and honey (to taste) and mix well.

2. Sprinkle cayenne in small pile on top of salad. Do not stir it in yet. Heat oil in small skillet over high heat. When it begins to smoke, add mustard seeds and cover with a lid or a splatter screen. As soon as the seeds stop sputtering, remove from heat and carefully pour oil over cayenne. Stir in dressing.

This sweet and tangy summer salad is always a hit at picnics and potlucks since it doesn't need to be refrigerated. The freshly "popped" mustard seeds give this dish a depth of flavor unique to any other dish on the table.

Malai Kofta

Prep Time: 15 minutes
Cook Time: 30 minutes
Serves 4

Ingredients:

For Kofta

- 2 ½ cups cottage cheese or grated semi-firm tofu
- ½ Tbsp. ginger garlic paste*
- 3-4 cashews, ground
- 4 green chilies, chopped
- 2 Tbsps. fresh coriander, chopped
- ½ Tbsp. ground cumin
- Salt, to taste
- 2 Tbsps. lemon juice
- 4 Tbsps. chickpea flour*

For Gravy

- 3 tsps. coconut or palm oil, divided
- 1 onion, finely chopped
- 1 tsp. turmeric powder
- 2 tsp. coriander powder
- ½ tsp. red chili powder
- 2 tomatoes, chopped
- Salt to taste
- 2 green chilies
- 2 cups coconut milk

Directions:

1. In a mixing bowl, knead cheese/tofu until it become smooth.

2. Add ginger garlic paste, cashews, green chilies, coriander, cumin, salt and lemon juice and mix well. Make small balls and roll them in chickpea flour.

3. Heat 2 teaspoons of oil in a skillet and sauté balls in batches turning frequently until they become golden brown in color.

4. Meanwhile, prepare gravy by sautéing onion in a separate skillet for 2-3 min using the remaining teaspoon of oil. Then add turmeric powder, coriander powder, red chili, green chilies, tomatoes and salt and simmer for 5 minutes until tomatoes become soft.

5. Add milk and over medium heat, bring mixture to a boil.

6. After a few minutes when gravy starts to thicken, add the kofta to the gravy and simmer for 5 more minutes.

   * To make your own chickpea flour: lightly toast dried chickpeas. Then grind into a fine powder using a food processor.

   * To make ginger garlic paste: Mince fresh garlic and ginger on a cutting board. Add a pinch of salt and using the back of a spoon or side of a knife, mash until a paste-like consistency forms.

With MalaiKofta, it's always celebration time! What a wonderful dish for special occasions or… anytime. The koftas themselves are so tasty, they can easily be served as a snack. This vegetarian alternative to meatballs goes very well with flatbread.

Pav Bhaji

Prep Time: 20 minutes
Cook Time: 30 minutes
Serves 4

Ingredients:

- 3 large potatoes, peeled and chopped to 1 inch pieces
- 3 cups mixed vegetables (a variety of carrots, cauliflower, peas. Can be bagged frozen vegetables for time saving)
- 2 Tbsps. coconut or palm oil
- 2 large onions, chopped
- 2 tsps. ginger garlic paste*
- 3 medium tomatoes, chopped
- 1-2 Tbsps. PavBhaji Masala
- 2 tsps. chili powder
- Salt, to taste
- 3-4 Tbsps. coriander leaves
- 1-2 Tbsps. ghee or butter

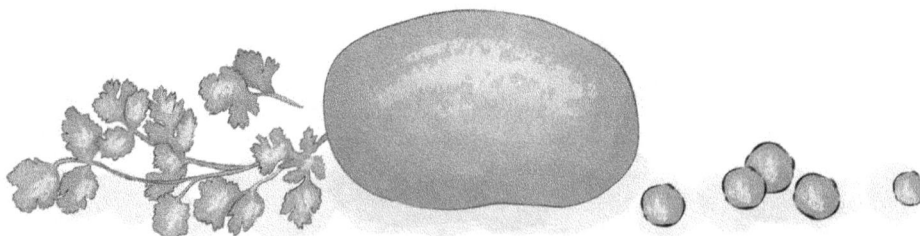

Directions:

1. In a large pot, place cubed potatoes with water just enough to cover potatoes and bring to a boil. Boil for 15 minutes and drain. With a potato masher or fork, mash potatoes roughly and set aside.

2. Cook the vegetables according to package directions. Mash them and set aside.

3. Meanwhile, heat oil in a wide pan. Add the onions and cook until they start to brown. Add the ginger garlic paste and cook for a minute more. Add the chopped tomatoes and cook until they are soft.

4. Add the pavbhaji masala, chili powder and salt. Cook for 2-3 minutes and then with a potato masher, mash the onion-tomato mixture until lumpy.

5. Add the mashed potatoes and vegetables. Mash thoroughly until the gravy becomes thick. You can add 1/4 cup of water at a time if the gravy appears to be dry before the veggies are mashed. You can keep mashing until the bhaji is totally smooth or you can stop when the veggies have been mashed to your level of preference. Adjust seasonings accordingly.

6. Add the chopped coriander leaves and ghee/butter; mix. Bhaji is ready to be served.

* To make ginger garlic paste: Mince the ginger and garlic on a cutting board and add a dash of salt. With the back of a spoon or side of a knife, mash the ginger and garlic with the salt until a paste-like consistency is formed.

It's definitely worth a trip to your local Asian Indian store for PavBhaji Masala. This special spice really brings out the flavor of this dish that is not only very popular in India but enjoyed by almost everyone. The Bhaji is traditionally served over toasted dinner rolls. For a healthier option, serve over sprouted whole grain bread.

Restaurant-Style Palak Paneer

Prep Time: 15 minutes
Cook Time: 30 minutes
Serves 4

Ingredients:

- 3 Tbsps. coconut oil, divided
- 2 cloves garlic, chopped
- 1 Tbsp. grated fresh ginger, divided
- 2 dried red chile peppers
- 1/2 cup finely chopped onion
- 3 tsps. ground cumin
- 2 tsps. ground coriander
- 1 tsp. ground turmeric
- 3/4 cup full-fa plain yogurt
- 2 (10 ounce) packages frozen spinach, thawed and drained
- 2 Tbsps. tomato paste + 2 Tbsps. water
- 4 sprigs fresh cilantro leaves
- 1 package paneer, sliced into small bite-size pieces
- Coarse sea salt to taste

Directions:

1. In a large saucepan heat 1 1/2 tablespoons of oil and sauté garlic, 1/2 tablespoon of ginger, red chilies and onion until brown. Mix in the cumin, coriander, turmeric and yogurt (add more or less to achieve desired creaminess).

2. Add the drained spinach and break spinach apart with your hands so it isn't one large clump. Sauté mixture for about 5 minutes and remove from heat. Allow to cool slightly.

3. Pour spinach mixture into a blender or food processor and add tomato paste, water, remaining 1/2 tablespoon of ginger, and cilantro (add more or less according to taste). Blend for 15 to 30 seconds. Pour back into the saucepan and keep warm over low heat.

4. In a medium skillet heat remaining 1 1/2 tablespoons of oil over medium heat, and sautépaneer, turning until browned.

5. Add paneer to spinach and cook for 10 minutes on low heat. Season with salt to taste.

Creamy, rich and a true delight to eat, Palak Paneer is one of the most popular vegetarian Indian paneer dishes. Basically, it is soft paneer or cottage cheese cubes cooked in a smooth spinach curry although there is nothing basic about the taste. If you have been craving this dish since last visiting your favorite Indian restaurant, now you can get your fix and make this restaurant–style version at home.

Roasted Eggplant Skillet

Prep Time: 15-30 minutes
Cook Time: 35 minutes
Serves 4

Ingredients:

- 2 medium eggplants
- 2 Tbsps. coconut oil
- 1 medium onion, sliced
- 1 tsp. chopped fresh ginger
- 3 clove garlic, minced
- 4 medium tomatoes; peeled, seeded and diced
- 1/2 tsp. each ground turmeric, ground cumin and ground coriander
- 1/4 tsp. cayenne pepper
- 1/2 tsp. each curry powder and salt
- Ground black pepper to taste
- 1/4 cup chopped fresh cilantro

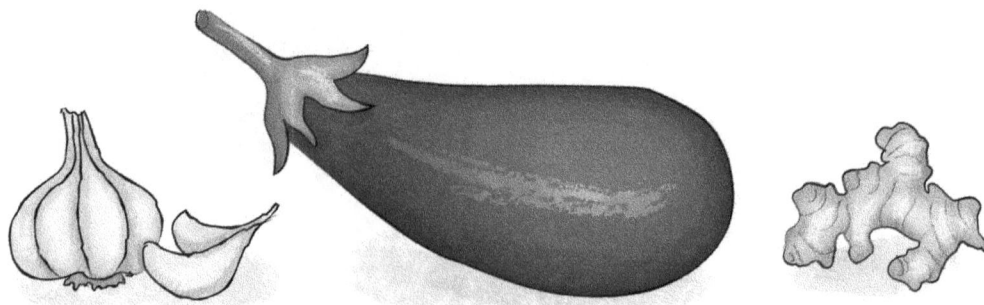

Directions:

1. Remove the skin on the eggplants and cut it into 1 inch rings, sprinkled with salt and let it sit for at 15-30 minutes (to remove the excess water). Dab rings with a dry paper towel.

2. Preheat broiler and spray rings lightly with cooking spray and arrange on lined baking sheet(s). Roast for approximately 15 minutes turning as needed for even cooking. Then cut eggplant rings into cubes. Set aside.

3. Meanwhile, heat the oil in a large skillet or wok over medium-high heat. Add the onion, ginger and garlic; cook and stir until tender. Stir in the tomatoes and season with turmeric, ground cumin, ground coriander, cayenne pepper, salt and black pepper. Cook and stir for a few minutes.

4. Place the eggplant pieces in the skillet, and cook for 10 to 15 minutes so some of the moisture evaporates. Taste, and adjust seasonings if desired. Garnish with fresh cilantro, and serve.

If you're looking for tasty ways to serve eggplant, this is the recipe for you. This one-skillet wonder will have you experiencing eggplant like you have never experienced it before. Eggplant naturally holds a lot of water and taking the time to complete the extra step of removing the excess moisture as described will give you a delightful flavor and consistency of eggplant that will have you using this method every time.

Shredded Carrot Raita Salad with Walnuts

Prep time: 5 minutes
Cook Time: 35 minutes (includes soaking time)
Serves 4

Ingredients:

- 2 Tbsps. raisins
- 1 1/2 cups plain Greek yogurt
- 1/2 tsp. honey
- 1/4 tsp. salt
- 1/4 tsp. ground cayenne or red pepper
- 1 Tbsp. finely chopped fresh mint leaves, divided
- 2 cups grated carrots (about 2 medium)
- 6 walnut halves, coarsely chopped

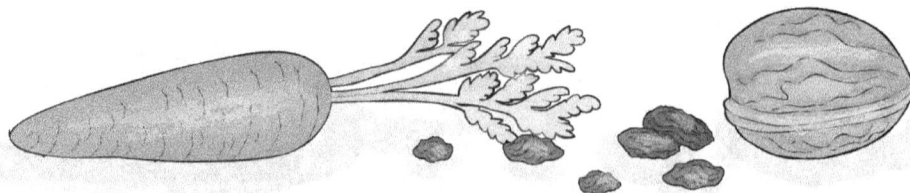

Directions:

1. Cover raisins with warm water in small bowl and soak at least 30 minutes or up to overnight.

2. Whisk together yogurt, honey, salt, cayenne (to taste), and 1/2 tablespoon of the mint in medium bowl. Add a few teaspoons of water if too thick.

3. Drain raisins and add to yogurt dressing along with carrots and walnuts. Stir well and sprinkle with the remaining 1/2 tablespoon mint.

This simple tangy yogurt-based dish makes a cooling accompaniment to your spicy main dishes. A hint of mint emphasizes the cooling action. Fear not if you have a dinner guest that tends to shy away from spicy dishes, this side dish will save the day and allow them to venture out into bold new territory!

Indian Spiced Cauliflower with Tomato Curry

Prep Time: 7 minutes
Cook Time: 30 minutes
Serves 4-6

Ingredients:

- 1 large head cauliflower
- 2 Tbsps. coconut oil, divided
- 1/2 tsp. ground turmeric
- 1 small onion, minced
- 2 tomatoes, pureed
- 1 tsp. garlic powder
- 3 tsps. garam masala
- 1/2 tsp. fresh ginger, minced
- Salt to taste
- 1/2 head lettuce

Directions:

1. Preheat the oven to 350 degrees F. Cut off most of the cauliflower's stem and cut head into small florets. Set aside.

2. Heat one tablespoon of oil and turmeric together in a small sauté pan. Toss the florets into the turmeric oil. Arrange florets on a lined baking sheet and bake the cauliflower florets for 30 minutes.

3. While the cauliflower is cooking heat remaining tablespoon of oil in a sauté pan, mix in the minced onions and sauté until medium brown in color. Add the pureed tomatoes, garlic powder, garam masala, ginger, and salt. Let this mixture simmer for 10 minutes.

4. Arrange lettuce leaves on a serving plate. Place the cauliflower on top of the lettuce. Pour the tomato curry over the cauliflower. Serve hot.

Roasted cauliflower is pretty tasty on its own. What happens when we roast it with a distinctive Indian spice such as turmeric? Sheer perfection! The perfect complement is the savory drizzle of tomato curry sauce all wrapped in a crisp lettuce leaf for one delicious bite after another.

Spicy Chickpea Sundal

Prep Time: 10 minutes
Cook Time: 15-20 minutes
Serves 3-4

Ingredients:

- 1 Tbsp. coconut oil
- 1/2 tsp. mustard seeds
- 1/4 tsp. red pepper flakes
- 1 string curry leaves (can be purchased at an Indian food specialty store or on Amazon. If you don't have this ingredient then omit, do not substitute. *Curry leaves are not the same as curry powder).
- 1/4 cup sweet onion, sliced lengthwise (optional)
- 1 can chickpeas, drained and rinsed
- Salt, to taste
- 2 Tbsps. unsweetened shredded coconut

Directions:

1. Heat the oil in a medium skillet over medium heat and add the mustard seeds, red chili flakes, and curry leaves- if using.

2. Sauté the onions until golden brown.

3. Add the chickpeas and required salt and sauté for 1 minute.

4. Add the shredded coconut. Toss everything together and remove from heat.

This simple and healthy snack is a common recipe in South India. This is a snack that is high in protein and filling. Kids will love it as an afternoon snack and adults will enjoy this tea time snack as well.

Spicy Indian Dahl

Prep Time: 10 minutes
Cook Time: 35 minutes
Serves 6

Ingredients:

- 1 cup red lentils
- 2 Tbsps. coconut oil
- 1 tsp. mustard seed
- 2 onions, chopped
- 2 Tbsps. fresh ginger, minced
- 3 jalapeno peppers, seeded and minced
- 6 cloves garlic, minced
- 1 tbsp. each ground cumin and ground coriander seed
- 4 tomatoes, chopped
- 2 Tbsps. fresh cilantro, finely chopped
- 1 cup vegetable broth

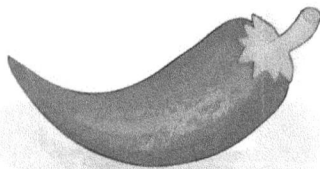

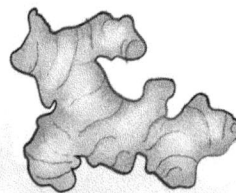

Directions:

1. Rinse and cook the lentils until they are soft according to package directions.

2. In a skillet over medium heat, heat the oil and add mustard seeds. When mustard seeds begin to flutter, add onions, ginger, jalapeno peppers, and garlic. Sauté until the onions and garlic are golden brown. Add cumin and coriander. Add chopped tomatoes. Sauté the mixture well until tomatoes are well cooked.

3. Add vegetable broth and cooked lentils. Boil for 6 minutes, stirring well. Add salt to taste, if needed.

4. Add finely chopped cilantro and remove from heat. Serve hot.

There's more than one way to cook up a mouthwatering pot of protein-rich lentils. This dish not only gives you several antioxidant vitamins from the lentils, it also packs in the flavor and a little heat for the perfect side dish or as a main course served with flatbread or naan. This isn't your average bowl of lentils!

Tofu Kadai Paneer

Prep Time: 10 minutes
Cook Time: 30 minutes
Serves 4-6

Ingredients:

- 1 block of semi- firmtofu; drained, patted dry, and cut into 1 inch cubes
- 3 Tbsps. coconut oil, divided
- 2 medium onions
- 2 Tbsps. tomato paste
- 8 cashew nuts
- 2 green chilies, slit lengthwise
- 1 tsp. each ginger paste and garlic paste
- 1 tsp. each turmeric powder, chili powder and salt
- 1 1/2 cups equal mix of peppers- red, yellow, and green bell pepper; cut into 1-1 1/2 inch strips
- 1 tsp. garam masala
- 1/2 cup peas
- Cilantro and julienned ginger for garnish

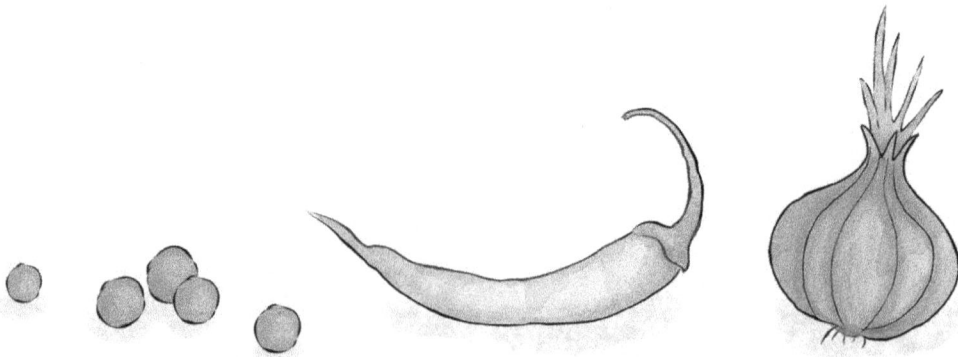

Directions:

1. Arrange the cubed tofu on a non-stick lined baking sheet and bake in 400 degree F oven for 5 minutes, just until the edges are starting to brown.

2. Heat 1 teaspoon oil in a pan and cube one of the onions and pan-roast onion until lightly browned. Add the tomato paste and cashews and sauté roast for another 2 minutes. In a food processor or stick blender, blend the onion and tomato paste along with cashew nuts into a paste. Add 1-2 tablespoons of water to help blend.

3. Thinly slice the remaining onion. Using the same pan, wipe dry and add remaining oil. Once hot, add sliced onions, green chilies and sautéuntil translucent.

4. Add ginger paste*, garlic paste*, turmeric, red chili powder, and 1 teaspoon salt and sauté for 2-3 minutes.

5. Now add all the peppers and cook on medium flame for 5-6 minutes or until just soft.

6. Add the onion-tomato-cashew paste and mix well to combine with the veggies and cook for another 4-5 minutes. You will see the oil from the cashews separating out. If preferred, add 1-2 tablespoons of water to thin out the gravy.

7. At this point add the garam masala. Taste and adjust seasonings as required.

8. Finally add the peas and tofu pieces and gently mix to combine them with the gravy. Close the lid and leave it on simmer for 5-6 minutes. Garnish with cilantro and julienned ginger and serve hot.

   * To make the paste: Mince the said ingredient, i.e. ginger or garlic, on a cutting board and add a dash of salt. With the back of a spoon or side of a knife, mash the ginger or garlic with the salt until a paste-like consistency is formed.

Kadai Paneer is a classic favorite of India. Paneer is a delicious dense cheese or cottage cheese cubes. We are adding a fun twist to this recipe for those who want to limit dairy without limiting flavor and texture. Tofu gives a wonderful consistency to keep the integrity of this dish while also providing a nice boost of protein.

Tomato Rasam

Prep Time: 15 minutes
Cook Time: 15 minutes
Serves 3

Ingredients:

- 2 tsps. coconut or palm oil
- 1/4 tsp. black mustard seeds
- 5 fresh curry leaves
- 1 large tomato, diced
- 1 tsp. cumin seed, finely ground
- 1/2 tsp. each ground black pepper and red pepper flakes
- 2 pinches ground dried turmeric
- 3 cloves garlic, crushed
- 3 cups water
- 2 tsps. tamarind paste
- Salt to taste
- 1 Tbsp. chopped fresh cilantro

Directions:

1. Heat the oil in a large saucepan over medium heat. Add the mustard seeds. As they start to sputter, add the curry leaves and tomato then season with cumin, pepper, red pepper flakes, turmeric and garlic.

2. Pour in the water and bring to a boil. Stir in tamarind paste, adjusting to taste if needed and season with salt. Simmer for about 2 minutes.

3. Ladle into bowls and garnish with cilantro to serve.

There are many varieties of rasam and a common favorite is the tomato rasam. This easy dish prepared in minutes can be served as a soup or along with brown rice. It's not only tasty but also soothing when suffering from a cold or fever.

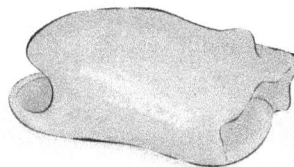

MEAT

Beef or Lamb Vindaloo

Prep Time: 15 minutes
Cook Time: 2 hours
Serves 4-6

Ingredients:

- 3 Tbsps. coriander
- 1 Tbsp. cumin
- 6 cloves
- 2 inches cinnamon sticks
- 1 tsp. each black peppercorns and fennel seed
- 2 tsps. fenugreek seeds(you can substitute this for curry powder or additional fennel seed)
- 1/4 cup white vinegar
- 4 -6 dried chilies, soaked
- 8 cloves garlic
- 1 large onion, roughly chopped
- 1 inch fresh ginger
- 2 pounds beef chuck steaks or 2 pounds lamb shoulder, trimmed and cut into 2 inch cubes
- 3 Tbsps. ghee or butter
- 2 bay leaves
- 2 cups beef stock

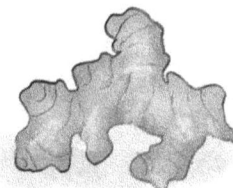

Directions:

1. Grind coriander, cumin, cloves, cinnamon, peppercorns, fenugreek and fennel to a fine powder using a coffee grinder or small food processor. Then mix spice powder with vinegar.
2. Place meat in container and rub well with spice mixture.
3. Using a food processor, grind chilies with garlic, onion and ginger to make a paste.
4. Pour chili paste over meat and marinate for at least 3 hours, or overnight.
5. Over high heat, heat ghee or butter in large heavy-bottom Dutch oven and sauté meat until deeply colored. Add bay leaves and stock and bring to a boil.
6. Reduce heat and simmer about 1 1/2- 2 hours, or until meat is very tender. Season to taste.

*This is one of those dishes that taste better the next day so if time permits, keep that in mind.

This dish originated in the Goa region of West India and keeping with the integrity of the dish we are seasoning with vinegar which also remains in most Indian interpretations today. The combination of spices compliments any meat you have on hand whether it be lamb, beef or chicken. Leftovers never tasted so good with this recipe so don't be shy if making a large batch.

Braised Chicken Curry

Prep Time: 10 minutes
Cook Time: 45 minutes
Serves 6

Ingredients:

- 2 Tbsps. coconut oil
- 2 medium yellow onions, finely chopped
- 4 large cloves garlic, finely grated
- 1 1/2 tsps. cayenne
- 1/2 tsp. ground turmeric
- 1/4 tsp. cumin seeds, finely ground
- 1 Tbsp. + 1 cup hot water, divided
- 3 medium tomatoes, finely chopped
- 3 pounds skinless chicken thighs and/or drumsticks
- 1/2 tsp. salt
- 1 Tbsp. apple cider vinegar
- 1 tsp. honey

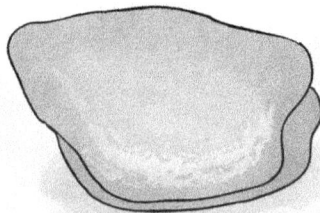

Directions:

1. Heat oil in large skillet over medium-high heat and sauté onion 10 minutes or until caramelized.

2. Combine garlic, cayenne, turmeric, and cumin in small bowl with 1 tablespoon of the water to make a thick paste. Add to onions and cook, stirring, about 5 minutes. Add tomatoes, reduce heat to medium, and cook, stirring to break up tomatoes, about 2 minutes (do not allow to scorch).

3. Add chicken and turn to coat with spice paste. Stir over medium heat 10 minutes. Add remaining 1 cup water and salt and bring to a boil. Reduce heat and simmer, uncovered, 30 minutes or until a thermometer inserted in the thickest part of chicken registers 165°F. Stir in vinegar and honey and simmer 1 minute.

Each cooking method has a way of bringing a different flavor to any dish. Chicken curry takes on a whole new experience with braising. Allowing the chicken to soak up all the flavor from the spices and vegetables makes for a tender dish with perfection in each bite.

Honey Curry Baked Chicken

Prep Time: 7 minutes
Cook Time: 55 minutes
Serves 6-8

Ingredients:

- 6-8 boneless, skinless chicken breasts
- 1/2 cup raw honey
- 1/2 cup ghee or butter, melted
- 1 Tbsp. curry powder
- 1 Tbsp. dry mustard
- 1/2 tsp. each lemon pepper and salt
- 1/4 tsp. garlic powder

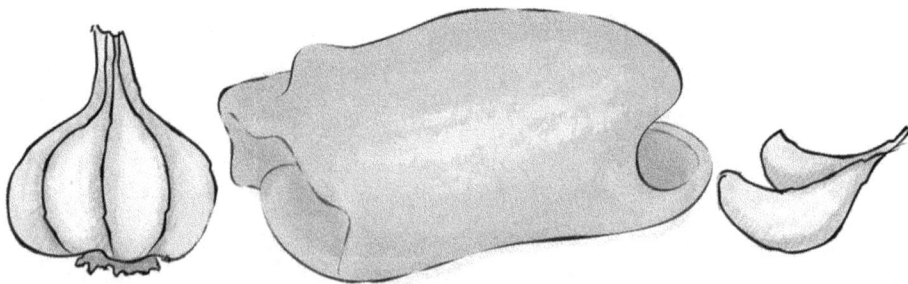

Directions:

1. Preheat oven to 350 degrees F.

2. Place chicken breasts in a 13x9 inch baking dish. Mix remaining ingredients together and pour over chicken.

3. Bake for 55 minutes and serve immediately as is or over coconut rice or quinoa.

If you've exhausted all of your chicken recipes, this is one sure to keep coming back again and again. There is no boredom with this dish when you combine the sweet honey coating along with the butter, curry and spices. Baked to perfection, you will think this chicken has been marinating for days.

Kadhai Murghi

Prep Time: 15 minutes
Cook Time: 20 minutes
Serves 4

Ingredients:

- 2 tsps. coriander seeds

- 1 tsp. each cumin seeds and fennel seeds

- 1 Tbsp. cornstarch

- 3/4 tsp. salt

- 1/2 tsp. ground turmeric

- 1 pound boneless, skinless chicken breasts, trimmed and cut into 1-inch cubes

- 2 Tbsps. coconut oil, divided

- 2 large carrots, cut into 1/4-inch-thick slices

- 1 large green bell pepper, cut into 1-inch cubes

- 1 small red onion, cut into 1/2-inch cubes

- 4 large cloves garlic, thinly sliced

- 3 dried red chiles, such as Thai, cayenne or chile de arbol, stemmed

- 1 Tbsp. lime juice

- 1/4 cup firmly packed fresh mint leaves, finely chopped

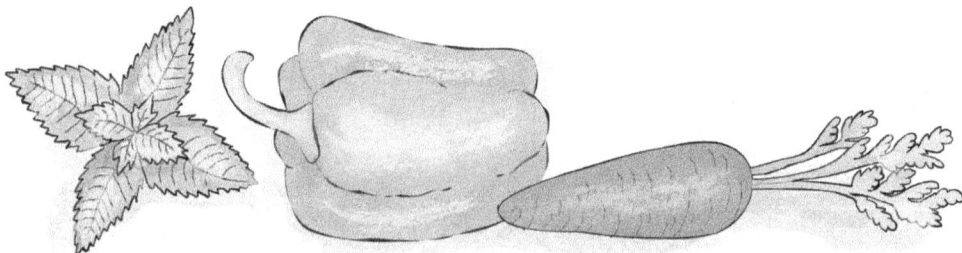

Directions:

1. Grind coriander, cumin and fennel seeds in a spice grinder or clean coffee grinder until the mixture resembles coarsely ground pepper. Transfer to a medium bowl and add cornstarch, salt and turmeric; stir to combine. Add chicken and stir until coated with the spice mixture.
2. Preheat a wok or a well-seasoned cast-iron skillet over high heat. Add 1 tablespoon oil. When the oil is shimmering, add carrots, bell pepper, onion, garlic and chiles. Cook, stirring, until the vegetables begin to brown, 4 to 6 minutes. Transfer to a plate.
3. Reduce heat to medium-high and add the remaining 1 tablespoon oil to the pan. Add the chicken and seasonings from the bowl and cook, stirring, until no longer pink in the middle, 5 to 7 minutes. Stir the vegetables and add lime juice and mint and cook until heated through, about 30 seconds.

This wok-seared chicken and vegetable dish brings you a colorful array of vegetables complimenting the spice-coated chicken. Enjoy the smoky aromas that spring from the pan and the combination of spices that entice the taste buds.

Kerala Beef Fry

Prep Time: 20 minutes
Cook Time: 50-55 minutes
Serves 4

Ingredients:

- 1 pound beef, cut into cubes
- 2 tsps. ground black pepper
- 1 tsp. each turmeric, chili powder and ground coriander and garam masala
- 2 tsp. garlic ginger paste*
- 1 medium tomato, chopped
- 2 green chiles, finely chopped
- 3 curry leaves
- 2 coriander leaves
- 1 medium onion, sliced
- 1 Tbsp. coconut oil

Directions:

1. Mix beef with black pepper, turmeric, chili powder, ground coriander, garam masala, ginger garlic paste, tomato and green chilies. Place beef with all the spices into a pressure cooker with very little water and let it cook for 2-3 "whistles" until the meat is tender. (Note: If you do not have a pressure cooker, cook in a large soup pot for about 40 minutes or until meat is tender.)

2. After the pressure comes down, open the cooker. Switch on the flame again.

3. Add fresh curry leaves, coriander leaves and sliced onions to the cooked beef and let it cook on medium-high heat until all the liquid evaporates.

4. Add oil little by little and continue frying until beef becomes dry and dark brown in color.

5. Serve the hot kerala beef fry with rice.

* To make ginger garlic paste: Mince fresh garlic and ginger on a cutting board. Add a pinch of salt and using the back of a spoon or side of a knife, mash until a paste-like consistency forms.

Kelara beef fry is served not just as a snack with friends visit but also as a main course dish with dosas. This delicious dish is a favorite in the South-Indian state of Kerala. With minimal ingredients and simple preparation, this is by far one of the better beef recipes that you'll try.

Lamb or Chicken Tikka Masala

Prep Time: 30 minutes
Cook Time: 50 minutes
Serves 4

Ingredients:

- 1 cup plain yogurt
- 1 Tbsp. lemon juice
- 4 tsps. ground cumin, divided
- 1 tsp. cinnamon
- 2 tsps. each cayenne pepper and freshly ground black pepper
- 1 Tbsp. minced fresh ginger
- 2 tsps. salt
- 3 boneless skinless chicken breasts, cut into bite-size pieces OR 1 1/2 pounds lamb stew meat
- 1 Tbsp. ghee or butter
- 1 clove garlic, minced
- 1 jalapeno pepper, finely chopped (remove seeds depending on your desired level of heat)
- 2 tsps. paprika
- 1 (8 ounce) can tomato sauce
- 1 cup coconut milk
- 1/4 cup chopped fresh cilantro

Directions:

1. In a large bowl, combine yogurt, lemon juice,2 teaspoons cumin, cinnamon, cayenne, black pepper, ginger, and salt. Stir in chicken/lamb, cover, and refrigerate for at least 1 hour.(If you have the time, marinating this all day adds extra flavor.)

2. Preheat a grill for high heat or heat oven to broil.

3. Lightly oil the grill grate if grilling or place a cookie rack over a foil-lined cookie sheet and spray with cooking spray if broiling. Thread chicken/lamb onto skewers if using a grill or just place chicken/lamb pieces directly on top of cookie rack. Discard marinade. Grill or broil until juices run clear, about 5 minutes on each side.

4. Meanwhile, melt ghee/butter in a large heavy skillet over medium heat. Sauté garlic and jalapeno for 1 minute. Season with remaining 2 teaspoons cumin and paprika. Stir in tomato sauce and coconut milk. Simmer on low heat until sauce thickens, about 20 minutes. Add grilled chicken, and simmer for 10 minutes. Transfer to a serving platter, and garnish with fresh cilantro.

Whether you love chicken tikka masala or you've never tried it before, you're in for a treat. This tremendously flavorful version is a must try. The yogurt helps tenderize the meat and the garlic, ginger and spices in this marinade infuse the meat with lots of flavor.

Mulligatawny

Prep Time: 20 minutes
Cook Time: 1 hour
Serves 6

Ingredients:

- 1/2 cup chopped onion
- 2 stalks celery, chopped
- 1 carrot, diced
- 1/4 cup ghee or butter
- 1 1/2 Tbsps. sprouted wheat/all-purpose flour
- 2 tsp. curry powder
- 4 cups chicken broth
- 1/2 apple, cored and shredded
- 1/4 cup rice
- 1 skinless, boneless chicken breast half, cut into cubes
- Salt and ground black pepper to taste
- 1 pinch dried thyme
- 1/2 cup coconut milk, heated or plain full-fat Greek yogurt

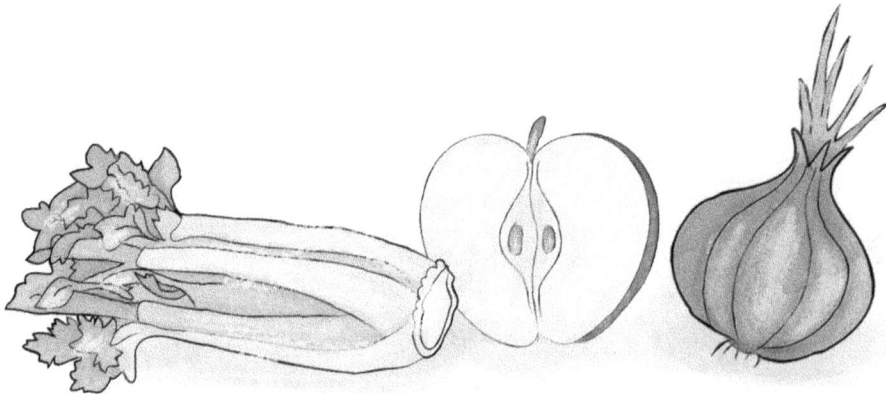

Directions:

1. Sauté onions, celery, carrot, and butter in a large soup pot. Add flour and curry, and cook 5 more minutes.

2. Add chicken broth, mix well, and bring to a boil. Simmer about 1/2 hour.

3. Add apple, rice, chicken, salt, pepper, and thyme. Simmer 20-25 minutes, or until rice is cooked.

4. When serving, add hot coconut milk or a dollop of yogurt on top of each serving.

This soup is full of vibrant flavor but is also warm and comforting. The name mulligatawny comes from 2 oriental Indian words meaning 'pepper water' but oh how this soup is so much more. Richly endowed with chicken and spices, this soup is thick and creamy and is almost more like a stew.

Spiced Lamb Seekh Kebobs

Prep Time: 15 minutes
Cook Time: 2 hours 10 minutes (includes marinating time)
Serves 8

Ingredients:

- 2 pounds lean ground lamb
- 2 onions, finely chopped
- 1/2 cup fresh mint leaves, finely chopped
- 1/2 cup cilantro, finely chopped
- 1 Tbsp. ginger paste
- 1 Tbsp. diced green chilies
- 2 tsps. each ground cumin, paprika, ground coriander
- 1 tsp. cayenne pepper
- 2 tsps. salt.
- Coconut oil for grill or skillet

Directions:

1. In a large bowl, mix ground lamb, onions, mint, cilantro, ginger paste*, and chiles. Season with cumin, coriander, paprika, cayenne, and salt. Cover, and refrigerate for 2 hours.

2. Mold handfuls of the lamb mixture, about 1 cup, to form sausages around skewers. Make sure the meat is spread to an even thickness. Refrigerate until you are ready to cook. Note: the kebabs will hold their shape better if allowed to rest in the refrigerator before cooking.

3. Preheat grill or skillet for high heat.

4. Brush grate liberally with oil, or place 1 tablespoon coconut oil in skillet. Arrange kabobs on grill or skillet. Cook for 10 minutes, or until well done, turning as needed to brown evenly.

   * To make ginger paste: Mince the ginger on a cutting board and add a dash of salt. With the back of a spoon or side of a knife, mash the ginger with the salt until a paste-like consistency is formed.

Who doesn't love meat on a stick? For your next BBQ, instead of the traditional dishes you would think of when firing up the grill, give these kebobs a whirl. A traditional meat used in India for kebabs is lamb and the flavor this dish gives when combined with this medley of spices will be sure to make your taste buds sizzle!

Tasty Tandoori Chicken

Prep Time: 10 minutes
Cook Time: 42 minutes (Includes marinating time)
Serves 4

Ingredients:

- 8 skinless, boneless chicken thighs (about 2 1/2 pounds)
- Juice of 1 lemon
- 2 tsps. Kosher salt, divided
- 1/2 cup plus 2 Tbsp. plain full-fat Greek yogurt
- 1 Tbsp. coconut oil, melted
- 1/2 small red onion, roughly chopped
- 3 cloves garlic, smashed
- 1 (2 inch) piece ginger, peeled and roughly chopped
- 4 tsps. tomato paste
- 2 tsps. ground coriander
- 1 1/2 tsps. ground cumin
- 1 3/4 tsps. paprika, divided
- 1/2 tsp. plus 1/8 teaspoon cayenne pepper
- 2 Tbsps. chopped fresh cilantro

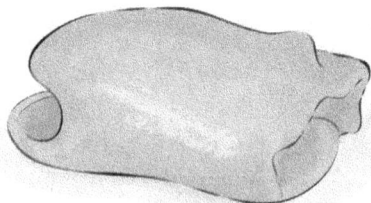

Directions:

1. Preheat the broiler. Make shallow cuts in the chicken thighs with a sharp knife. In a large bowl, toss the chicken with the lemon juice and 1 1/2 teaspoons salt.
2. Pulse 2 tablespoons yogurt, the coconut oil, onion, garlic, ginger, tomato paste, coriander, cumin, 11/2 teaspoons paprika and 1/2 teaspoon salt in a food processor to make a paste. Toss the chicken in the mixture and let marinate in the refrigerator for 30 minutes.
3. Place the chicken on a foil-lined broiler pan. Broil, turning once, until slightly charred and a thermometer inserted into the center registers 165 degrees F; 5 to 6 minutes per side.
4. Meanwhile, combine the remaining 1/2 cup yogurt and 1/4 teaspoon paprika, 1/8 teaspoon cayenne, the cilantro and a pinch of salt in a bowl. Top the chicken with the yogurt sauce.

This popular Indian dish is known for bold flavor and spice. A light marinade in a spicy yogurt sauce gives this chicken a tender texture and flavor. Topped with a spiced yogurt topping, this dish not only tastes the part, but has a beautiful presentation as well.

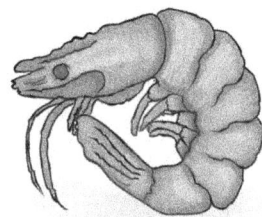

Seafood

Coconut Curry Shrimp

Prep Time: 5 minutes
Cook Time: 20 minutes
Serves 4

Ingredients:

- 1 Tbsp. coconut oil
- 1/2 sweet onion, minced
- 2 cloves garlic, chopped
- 1 tsp. each ground ginger and ground cumin
- 1 1/2 tsps. ground turmeric
- 1 tsp. paprika
- 1/2 tsp. chili powder
- 1 (14.5 ounce) can chopped tomatoes
- 1 (14 ounce) can coconut milk
- 2 Tbsps. crushed cashews
- 1 tsp. salt
- 1 pound cooked and peeled shrimp
- 2 Tbsps. chopped fresh cilantro

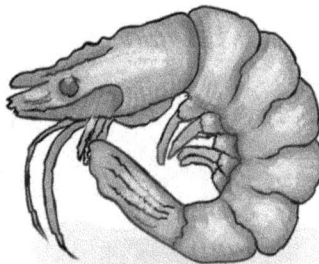

Directions:

1. Heat the oil in a large skillet over medium heat; cook the onion in the hot oil until translucent, about 5 minutes.

2. Remove the skillet from the heat and allow it to cool slightly, about 2 minutes. Add the garlic, ginger, cumin, turmeric, paprika, and chili powder to the onion and stir over low heat.

3. Pour the tomatoes, coconut milk, and cashews into the skillet; season with salt. Cook the mixture at a simmer, stirring occasionally, about 10 minutes.

4. Stir the shrimp and fresh cilantro into the sauce mixture; cook another 1 minute before serving.

This is a quick and easy dish served conveniently for a weeknight dinner that is so satisfying. The sweetness of the coconut milk with the savory mix of curry spices pair together wonderfully for a go-to meal every time.

Curried Salmon and Eggplant

Prep Time: 15 minutes
Cook Time: 20 minutes
Serves 4

Ingredients:

- 1 Tbsp. coconut oil
- 1 Tbsp. plus 1 tsp. yellow curry paste or 1 tsp. curry powder, or to taste
- 2 cloves garlic, minced
- 1 medium eggplant, (about 1 pound), cut into 1/2-inch cubes
- 1 (14-ounce) can light coconut milk
- 1 Tbsp. plus 1 tsp. fish sauce
- 1 Tbsp. finely ground coconut sugar
- 1 pound skinned salmon fillet, cut into 1-inch pieces
- 2 cups sugar snap peas, trimmed
- 1/2 cup chopped fresh basil
- 3 Tbsps. lime juice

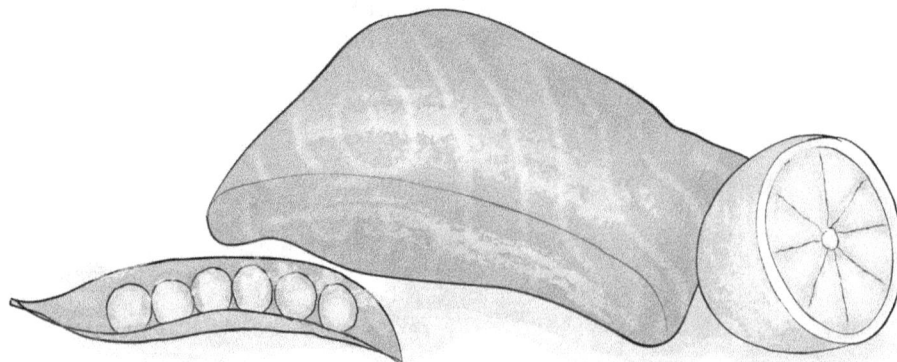

Directions:

1. Heat oil in a large skillet over medium heat. Add curry paste/powder and garlic and cook, stirring, until fragrant, about 1 minute. Add eggplant and cook, stirring, until the eggplant is coated with the curry mixture and softened, about 7 minutes.

2. Add coconut milk, fish sauce and coconut sugar to the pan. Bring to a boil; stir in salmon and snow peas. Reduce heat to a simmer, cover and cook, stirring occasionally, until the salmon is cooked through and the peas are tender-crisp, about 5 minutes. Remove from the heat. Stir in basil and lime juice.

Teamwork has never tasted so good! Salmon and eggplant pair up deliciously to bring you this one-skillet curry flavored with coconut milk, basil and lime. Yellow curry paste, found in the Asian section of the supermarket, is an aromatic blend of Thai flavors that includes chilies, shallots, lemongrass, galangal, lime and turmeric. Get ready to wow your dinner guests with this dish full of flavor.

Mango Basil Shrimp

Prep Time: 15 minutes
Cook Time: 35 minutes (includes marinating time)
Serves 4

Ingredients:

- 1 pound raw shrimp, (21-25 per pound), peeled and deveined, tails left on
- 1/4 tsp. salt
- 1/4-1/2 tsp. cayenne pepper
- 1/4 tsp. ground turmeric
- 1 Tbsp. coconut oil
- 2 large ripe, firm mangos, peeled and cut into 1/2-inch cubes
- 1 bunch scallions, green tops only, thinly sliced
- 1/4 cup firmly packed fresh basil leaves, finely chopped

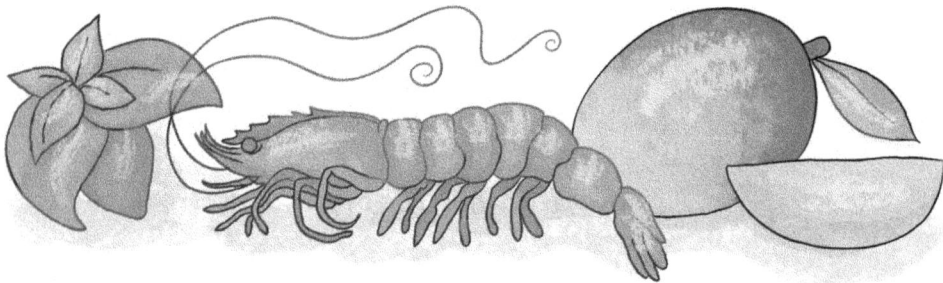

Directions:

1. Toss shrimp with salt, cayenne to taste and turmeric in a medium bowl. Cover; refrigerate for about 30 minutes.

2. Heat oil in a large nonstick skillet over medium-high heat; place the shrimp in a single layer and cook until the undersides turn salmon-pink, about 1 minute. Flip them over and cook for 1 minute more.

3. Add mango, scallions and basil and cook, stirring, until the shrimp is just cooked and starts to barely curl, 1 to 2 minutes.

Ready to evoke dinner-time 'oohs' and 'ahhs'? This one-pan dish is an Indian feast that will do just that. Sweet shrimp, fragrant mangos and spicy basil make for a delicious fiery dish. To make prep time even more of a breeze, use pre-peeled shrimp.

Spice Rubbed Salmon

Prep Time: 12 minutes
Cook Time: 10 minutes
Serves 2

Ingredients:

- 2 cups water
- 1 Tbsp. + 1/2 tsp. Kosher salt
- 2 (4 ounce) salmon fillets
- 1 1/2 tsps. ground turmeric
- 2 Tbsps. ground coriander
- 1 1/2 tsps. paprika
- 1 Tbsp. coconut oil
- 1 sprig cilantro

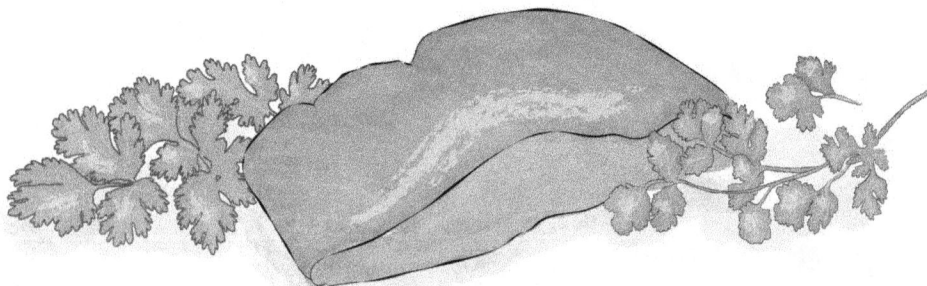

Directions:

1. Combine the water and 1 tablespoon salt in a shallow container. Soak the salmon in the salt water for 10 minutes.

2. Mix the turmeric, coriander, paprika, and 1/2 teaspoon salt in a small bowl. Remove salmon from the salt water and pat dry with paper towels. Coat salmon on both sides with spice mixture.

3. Heat the oil in a small skillet over medium heat. Cook salmon in hot oil for 5 minutes per side. Serve garnished with cilantro.

Salmon is pretty tasty on its own and with this Indian spice medley, what better way to receive your Omega 3 serving than with this dish. Ready in minutes, this appetizing dish can be served for 2 or scaled up for a crowd... without adding to your prep and cook time!

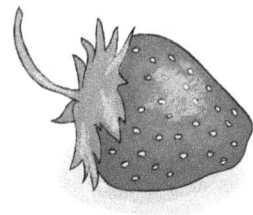

Sweets and Breads

Banana Dosai (Banana Pancakes)

Prep Time: 10 minutes
Cook Time: 15 minutes
Serves 2-4

Ingredients:

- 2 ripe bananas
- 1/4 cup almond flour
- 2 Tbsps. sprouted whole wheat/all-purpose flour
- Coconut sugar, to taste
- Pinch of cardamom powder
- 2 Tbsps. raisins, chopped
- 2 Tbsps. cashews, chopped
- 1 Tbsp. ghee, divided

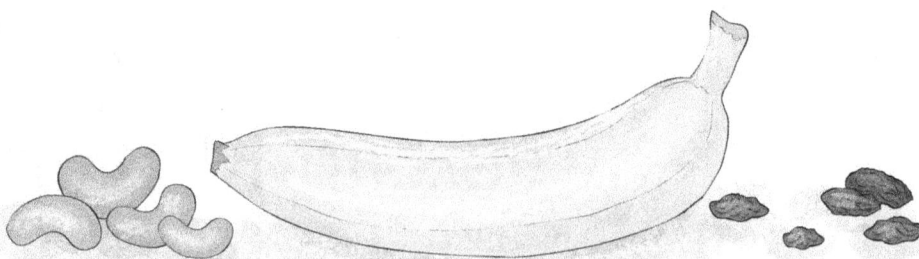

Directions:

1. Mash the bananas with a masher or fork.

2. Add almond flour, sprouted whole wheat/all-purpose flour, coconut sugar and cardamom powder. Mix everything together to make a thick batter.

3. Mix in the raisins and cashews to the batter.

4. Heat a griddle over medium heat and melt 1 teaspoon of Ghee to evenly coat griddle. Pour batter by the spoonful and spread each cake gently.

5. Pour a few drops of ghee on top. Cook until the dosa is completely cooked and golden brown on both sides- usually a few minutes per side.

These crispy pancakes from South India are a staple in its home region as in the rest of the country too. Bursts of sweetness from the raisins and a crunch from the cashews makes these filling banana dosas ready to consume without any extras.

Besan Halwa

Prep Time: 5 minutes
Cook Time: 30 minutes
Serves 8

Ingredients:

- 1 cup milk or coconut milk
- 1/2 cup water
- 1/2 tsp. ground cardamom
- 1/4 tsp. ground cinnamon
- 3/4 cup ghee
- 1 cup chickpea four*
- 1 cup finely ground coconut sugar

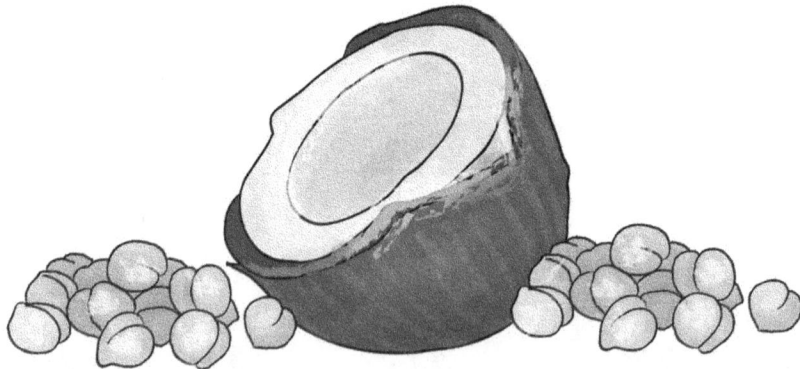

Directions:

1. Bring the milk and water to a simmer in a saucepan over medium-low heat; stir the cardamom and cinnamon into the mixture. Set aside.

2. Melt the ghee in a shallow skillet over medium heat; stir the chickpea flour into the melted ghee and cook until fragrant and just browned, about 10 minutes.

3. Add the sugar and stir to incorporate. Slowly pour the milk mixture into the skillet while stirring to avoid lumps. Continue cooking and stirring until the halwa pulls away from the sides of the pan, 10 to 15 minutes. Serve hot or spread the mixture into a rimmed plate and allow to cool. Cut into squares and serve.

*To make your own chickpea flour: lightly toast dried chickpeas. Then grind into a fine powder using a food processor.

Devoured by all sweets lovers, you may gobble this up before it has a chance to cool down! This rich and delicious Indian dessert is very easy and quick to prepare. Chickpea flour is relatively higher in protein than other flours and for anyone with gluten sensitivity, this dessert appeals to many.

Makkai Ki Roti
(Griddle-Cooked Organic Corn Flatbread)

Prep Time: 10 minutes
Cook Time: 1 hour
Makes 12 flatbreads

Ingredients:

- 2 cups finely ground yellow corn flour or masa harina
- 1/2 cup sprouted wheat/all-purpose flour
- 3/4 tsp. salt
- 4 (1/4-inch thick) slices fresh ginger
- 2-4 fresh serrano chiles, stemmed
- 1/2 cup finely chopped red onion
- 1/4 cup finely chopped fresh cilantro
- 1-1 1/4 cups warm water
- 1 Tbsp. ghee, or butter, melted
- 1 Tbsp. melted coconut oil or palm oil

Directions:

1. Combine corn flour, sprouted flour and salt in a medium bowl.

2. Pulse ginger and chiles in a food processor until minced. Add to the flour mixture along with onion and cilantro.

3. Drizzle warm water over the mixture, a few tablespoons at a time, stirring it in as you go, until the mixture starts to come together and form a ball. Turn the dough out onto a lightly floured surface. Gently knead until a soft dough forms (it will still be a little lumpy from the vegetables). Divide the dough into 12 portions and shape each into a ball. Keep the balls covered with plastic wrap or with a slightly damp paper towel.

4. Fold a large sheet of foil in half lengthwise. Combine ghee and oil in a small bowl and set aside next to the stove.

5. Coat a small nonstick skillet with cooking spray and heat over medium heat. Place a ball of dough between sheets of wax paper (leaving the others covered). Press it down to form a patty, then roll it out into a 1/8-inch-thick disc, 4 to 6 inches in diameter (the edges won't be perfectly round and will appear jagged and cracked). Gently peel the dough off the paper and add it to the hot pan. Cook until the underside is light brown in spots, 1 to 2 minutes. Flip it over and cook for 1 to 2 minutes more. Brush the top with butter-oil mixture and flip it over to sear it, about 30 seconds. Brush the second side with butter-oil mixture and flip it over to sear that side too, about 30 seconds. Slip the bread into the foil sleeve to keep warm.

6. Repeat with the remaining dough. Serve warm.

This classic Punjabi corn meal flatbread is spiced with green chilies, ginger and other fragrant flavors making it a welcome accompaniment for most dishes or served with a dip for an appetizer. While making flatbread using corn flour may seem a little out of the ordinary for some people, it is used because corn is grown to a large extent all over Northern India and thrives particularly well in Punjab. Hence, Punjab's traditional and classic combination was created.

Shahi Anjir Coconut Ice Cream

Prep Time: 20 minutes
Cook Time: 20 minutes + at least 3 hours of freeze time
Serves 4-6

Ingredients:

- 3 Tbsps. ghee or butter

- 1/3 cup + 2 Tbsps. coconut sugar ground to a fine powder, divided

- 1 cup fresh figs chopped into tiny pieces

- 2 egg whites

- 1 3/4 cup full-fat canned coconut milk

- 1/2 tsp. vanilla extract

- 4-5 Tbsps. honey

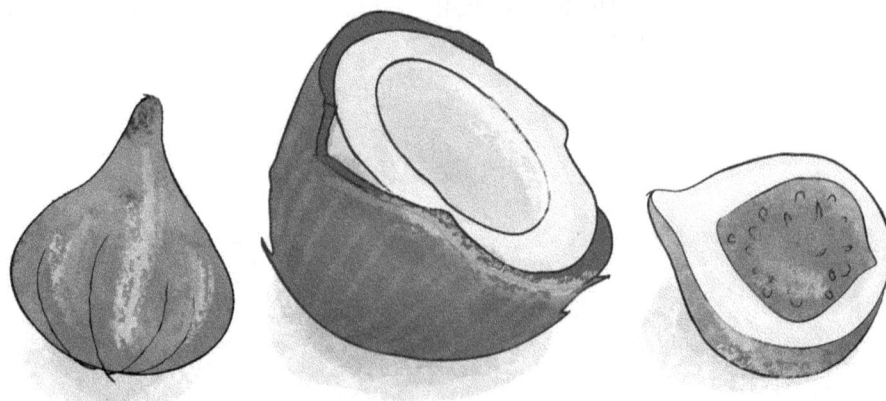

Directions:

1. Heat a pan on medium heat until hot. Add the ghee/butter and allow to melt. Add 2 tablespoons coconut sugar and figs to the pan and stir well. Cook until the figs are soft, stirring frequently. Remove from heat and allow to cool completely. Keep aside for later use.

2. Whisk egg whites in a clean, dry bowl, until they get fluffy and soft peaks form.

3. In a separate bowl, whisk the coconut milk, coconut sugar and vanilla extract together until well incorporated.

4. Add the fig mixture to the coconut milk mixture and blend with a wooden spoon.

5. Gently fold this mixture into the egg whites. Once fully blended, pour into a freezer bowl and cover.

6. Freeze for 3 hours or until firm. Remove from the freezer and mix with a wooden spoon again until smooth. Drizzle the honey in swirls over the mixture and gently fold into it.

7. Place back in the freezer until firm again. Scoop out into individual bowls and serve.

"You scream, I scream, we all scream for ice cream." And this recipe is no different! Very popular in India and dressed to impress, this ice cream will do just that. Simple and tasty with swirls of honey throughout, you'll be smiling with every bite.

Strawberry Lassi

Prep Time: 2 minutes
Cook Time: 5 minutes
Serves 1

Ingredients:

- 1 cup plain full-fat yogurt
- 1 cup cold water
- Honey, as needed
- 1/2 tsp. vanilla extract
- Pinch of cardamom powder
- 2/3 cup sliced fresh strawberries

Directions:

1. Blend all the above ingredients together using a blender until it becomes frothy.

2. Garnish with fresh mint leaves and serve as a cool, healthy and refreshing drink.

Lassi is a popular, traditional, yogurt-based drink enjoyed throughout India. This concoction is ready to cool you down in the summer or serve as a refreshing dessert. The beautiful thing about this recipe is its versatility. Substitute equal parts of the strawberry with mango, banana, or any other flavor you desire.

Ben Hirshberg is a young author, health consultant, and entrepreneur from Seattle. His main topics of interest are positive psychology, behavioral psychology, personal finance, entrepreneurship, nutrition, and anything else health related. He likes to cook, meditate, read, party, and go trail running. Ben is certified as a personal trainer by WITS and as a fitness nutrition specialist by NASM.

Download the Eudaimonia Manifesto for FREE at www.BenHirshberg.com.

Creator of www.RecipesForRadiance.com, Jessica Robinsonis a fun-loving home cook. She revamps some of our favorite guilty pleasures into healthier, time-saving alternatives that incorporate specific nutrient-packed ingredients. Jessica has been a contributor for the healthy cooking segment on a popular women's online platform. Recipes for Radiance was also showcased in the debut issue of HER (Hardworking-Empowered-Resilient) magazine.

www.ingramcontent.com/pod-product-compliance
Lightning Source LLC
Chambersburg PA
CBHW080551030426
42337CB00024B/4837